THE FARMINGTON COMMUNITY LIBRARY
FARMINGTON BRANCH
23500 Liberty Street
Farmington, MI 48335-3570

JAN 3 1 2002

John Adams

by
Stuart A. Kallen

Visit us at
www.abdopub.com

Published by ABDO Publishing Company, 4940 Viking Drive, Edina, MN 55435. Copyright ©2001 by Abdo Consulting Group, Inc. International copyrights reserved in all countries. No part of this book may be reproduced in any form without written permission from the publisher.

Printed in the United States.

Graphic Design: John Hamilton
Cover Design: MacLean Tuminelly

Cover photo: Corbis
Interior photos and illustrations:
   Abby Aldrich Rockefeller Folk Art Center, p. 9
   American Antiquarian Society, p. 30
   Corbis, p. 6-7, 8, 11, 13, 17, 19, 20, 23, 29, 41, 43, 47, 51, 57
   Harvard Portrait Collection, p. 27
   Independence National Historical Park, p. 55
   John Hamilton, p. 31, 39
   Library of Congress, p. 25, 26, 33, 35, 37, 49
   Massachusetts Historical Society, p. 15
   National Portrait Gallery, Smithsonian Institution, p. 5
   National Park Service, Adams National Historic Site, p. 59
   New York Historical Society, p. 53

   Library of Congress Cataloging-in-Publication Data
Kallen, Stuart A., 1955-
   John Adams / Stuart A. Kallen.
     p. cm. — (The founding fathers)
   Includes index.
   Summary: A biography of the lawyer from Braintree, Massachusetts, who became an important public figure in early American history and the second president of the United States.
   ISBN 1-57765-007-7
   1. Adams, John, 1735-1826—Juvenile literature.
2. Presidents—United States—Biography—Juvenile literature.
[1. Adams, John, 1735-1826 2. Presidents.]   I. Title.

E322.K35 2001
973.4'4'092—dc21
[B]
                                98-010816

Contents

Introduction 4
Puritan Farmers 8
Schooling and Skipping 10
Student to Teacher 12
Lawyer to the Revolution 14
Trade, Tariffs, and Searches 16
Family Matters 22
Stopping the Stamp Act 24
The Redcoats Arrive 28
Massacres and Tea Parties 32
The First Continental Congress 36
The Minutemen 40
The Declaration of Independence 42
Off to France 44
The Diplomat 46
The First Vice-President 48
The Second President 50
Troubles in Office 52
Retirement 54
Death of a President 56
Conclusion 58
Timeline 60
Where on the Web? 61
Glossary 62
Index 64

Introduction

ON MARCH 4, 1797, the United States of America was less than 10 years old, however, the country was facing a major problem. France and England were at war. The European nations were threatening America, and both countries wanted to drag the young country into their war. John Adams had just been sworn in as the country's second president. There was no honeymoon period for him to adjust to the new job. Something had to be done—and soon.

France refused to talk to American peace agents, and they threatened to seize all American ships and their cargo. If American seamen were found on English ships, France would hang them. President Adams rose before Congress to press for more money. America needed a stronger navy, a stronger military, and three peace agents to negotiate with France. Congress wasn't interested in the president's proposals.

Facing page: A portrait of President John Adams.

Americans were sharply divided over which country to fight. There were two political parties, the Federalists and the Republicans. The Federalists, from the northern states, sided with England. The Republicans, from the southern states, sided with France. Adams wanted to keep the country neutral and peaceful. This made him a target for both political parties.

At the age of 61, the short, stout Adams was tired of the squabbling. The political attacks left him weary. But he believed that public service was a noble calling. As a young man, he had written, "The only principles of public conduct worthy of a gentleman... are to sacrifice ease, health, applause,

The Battle of the Nile was fought between the British and Napoleon's French fleets in Abukir Bay, near Alexandria, Egypt, on August 1, 1798. It was one of the greatest victories for the British, under Admiral Horatio Nelson. Americans and their political leaders were sharply divided over who to support during the war between the French and British.

and even life itself to the sacred calls of his country." With these words to guide him, John Adams knew that he must fight on. Once again, he put his own comfort aside for the good of the country he loved so dearly.

John Adams   7

Puritan Farmers

JOHN ADAMS COULD TRACE his strong, sturdy roots back to 1638. That's when his great-great-grandfather Henry Adams first arrived in Massachusetts. Henry was a religious man, a Puritan who came to America to escape religious persecution in England. The Adams family soon settled on a small farm in Braintree, on the coastal road between Boston and Plymouth. That's where John Adams was born on October 30, 1735.

"Puritans Walking to Church," by George Barrie.

As John was growing up, he loved to spend his time on the rocky pastures of his parents' farm. He helped chop wood, carry water from the well, milk the cows, and work the fields of barley and wheat. When John grew up, he wanted to be a farmer, just like his father and grandfather before him.

On Sundays the family would spend all day at the Puritan church. The Puritans were simple people who believed in a very strict form of Christianity.

John's father was a man with little education. But he was a church deacon, tax collector, constable, and militia officer. John's mother came from a cultured and well-educated Massachusetts family. She was talkative, emotional, and hard working. She passed these traits along to John.

A prosperous New England farm, painted by Edward Hicks, an artist and preacher.

Schooling and Skipping

BOTH OF JOHN'S PARENTS wanted him to have a good education. John learned to read when he was very young. When he was a little older, he joined the other children of Braintree in a one-room schoolhouse. There he studied reading, writing, and arithmetic.

A one-room schoolhouse like the one John Adams attended in Braintree, Massachusetts.

10 Founding Fathers

Cambridge, Massachusetts.

John continued his education through his teen years, but he quarreled with his father, arguing that he only wanted to be a farmer. Still, at 15, the young man went to Cambridge, Massachusetts. There, he passed the difficult test to gain admission to Harvard College.

Student to Teacher

TO PAY FOR JOHN'S COLLEGE education, his father sold 30 acres (12 hectares) of farmland. Two months before his 16th birthday, John set off to college. He wanted to study for the ministry.

John studied hard at Harvard. He began to read through the school's 3,500-book library. Some books made him question whether he wanted to be a minister. He had doubts about church doctrines. He felt ministers preached too narrow a view of religion. He discussed his doubts with his science teacher, who suggested that John teach for a year or two. When John graduated he was third in his class. He was offered a job as a schoolmaster in Worcester, Massachusetts.

Facing page: A view of Harvard College (later University) around the time John Adams attended.

Lawyer to the Revolution

JOHN ADAMS WAS 20 years old in 1755. He began teaching Latin to children in Worcester. The town had about 1,500 people, many of them were eager to meet the bright, young Harvard graduate. Adams was invited to dinners and parties. There he met lawyers who talked of politics and world events. Talk usually centered on England and France. The two European countries had been fighting for 50 years over land borders in America.

As the months wore on, Adams began to dislike teaching. Over the protests of his parents, Adams decided to become a lawyer. In earlier times, Puritans believed lawyers were doing the work of the devil. By 1755, however, the war between England and France was creating a demand for lawyers. Business was booming. There was a demand for contracts in shipping, lumber, fishing, and land speculation.

In large towns like Boston, lawyers were elected as government officials. Successful lawyers were well known. Adams decided to make a name for himself. He taught school until he had enough money to study law and start a practice in Boston.

Adams studied with a Worcester lawyer named James Putnam. He copied wills, wrote deeds, prepared court briefs, and argued court cases. On October 1, 1758, John Adams became a practicing lawyer.

Adams went back to the family farm in Braintree. He opened his law office in his parents' living room. He also attended town meetings, where he helped guide Braintree government. In 1761, Adams was chosen as a city council member.

John Adams as a young lawyer.

John Adams 15

Trade, Tariffs, and Searches

ENGLAND WON ITS WAR against France in 1760. French troops left North America for the first time in 70 years. Americans were relieved. The Adams family celebrated with a day of prayer and fasting. But new problems were on the horizon.

England's King George III felt that his country was losing money to the Americans. Americans were trading with the French, Spanish, and Dutch. King George wanted to profit from this trade. England needed the money to pay for its costly war against France.

England ordered Americans to pay tariffs, or taxes, on imported goods. Boston businessmen felt the taxes would ruin them. To avoid paying, they disguised their cargo. They unloaded boats secretly at night, and bribed customs officials who were supposed to collect the tariffs.

Facing page: England's King George III.

The English fought back. They gave customs officials search warrants. This allowed the officials to search for smuggled goods in a colonist's home, ship, office, or warehouse. As English citizens, Americans believed they had protection against these searches.

The taxes and tariffs were passed down from England's governing body, called the Parliament. The colonists thought if England was going to tax them, they should have representatives in the Parliament. The colonist motto was "No taxation without representation."

Facing page: State Opening of Parliament, England. Each autumn, usually in November, the Queen travels to the House of Lords to open the new parliamentary session in the State Opening of Parliament ceremony.

20 Founding Fathers

In 1761, John Adams was working with a lawyer named James Otis. Boston merchants hired Otis to argue their case in court against the tax collectors. This was the first battle between King George and the colonists.

The courtroom was very crowded. Adams had to shove his way in to a seat. Otis argued for five hours. He said colonists would not tolerate high-handed actions from England. He said, "A man who is quiet and orderly is as secure in his house as a prince in his castle."

Adams was so excited by the speech he forgot to take notes. When he returned to Braintree, he wrote, "Then and there the child of Independence was born!" The case was decided in favor of England. But the seeds of revolution had been planted.

Facing page: Boston's Old State House, the site where James Otis gave his speech against the British Writs of Assistance, which gave the British the right to search the homes and businesses of anybody they suspected of violating tax laws.

Family Matters

IN MAY 1761, JOHN'S father died from influenza at the age of 70. John inherited 10 acres (four hectares) of the family farm. At the age of 26, he had a successful law practice and owned land. But he was lonely and wanted a wife.

John had known Abigail Smith since she was 13. At their first meeting, he thought she was shy. She thought he was stubborn and argued too much. Abigail had been too frail to go to school. Her father taught her at home. It was not fashionable for girls at the time to have an education. But Abigail was an avid reader and quick learner.

By the age of 17, Abigail Smith was a graceful woman with a bright mind. John asked Abigail's father for her hand in marriage. Mrs. Smith was hoping for a richer son-in-law from a better family. She stalled the wedding, saying Abigail was too frail to marry. John waited patiently.

Finally, three years later, on October 25, 1764, John and Abigail were married. She wore a red and white woolen dress and new cloak. He wore a white wig tied back and a dark blue satin waistcoat embroidered with gold thread. People thought they were a perfect couple.

A portrait of Abigail Adams by Benjamin Blythe.

Stopping the Stamp Act

AFTER THE MARRIAGE, the Adamses settled on John's farm. The lawyer's marriage to well-to-do Abigail had improved his social standing. Wealthy and powerful Bostonians sought his council.

By 1765, tensions had grown between England and the colonies. Parliament passed the Stamp Act. This required people to buy official royal stamps for every legal document. Adams felt this would ruin the law business. Boston flags were lowered to half-mast and church bells tolled in mourning. Bostonians began to organize.

John's cousin, Samuel Adams, organized merchants and craftspeople into a revolutionary party called the Sons of Liberty.

Facing page: The Stamp Act riots in Boston.

In August, an angry mob attacked and looted the lieutenant governor's house. They hung and burned an effigy of the local stamp seller in an old elm tree. John was against the taxes, but hated mob violence. He decided to protest by writing many newspaper articles.

Meanwhile, the Adams family had a new addition, a girl also named Abigail. As Abigail attended to the newborn, John wrote a long essay on English law and published it in the *Boston Gazette* newspaper. He believed in the idea of dividing the government into three branches. The legislative branch would make laws. The executive branch would carry out the laws. The judicial branch would settled disputes about what the laws meant.

Adams organized citizens, who sent a message to the Massachusetts legislature claiming that the Stamp Tax was illegal. Soon Adams was in court arguing against the Parliament's right to tax the colonies. England lost the fight. They repealed the Stamp Act one year after it was passed. Adams celebrated the victory.

Left: An American cartoon showing opposition to the Stamp Act.

A portrait of John Adams, by John Singleton Copley.

The Redcoats Arrive

ADAMS HAD A GROWING family to feed. He decided to move to Boston so he could make more money. The Adamses moved into a white house on Boston's Brattle Square. Boston was noisy and crowded compared to the quiet farm. But the Adamses could spend more time together with their newest child John Quincy.

Samuel Adams brought John clients who supported the Sons of Liberty. The English governor of Massachusetts thought so much of Adams's talents that he offered him a job in the British-run courts. Adams thought that the money would help his family. But he was too dedicated to the cause of liberty. He could not be bribed by the other side.

A 1722 map showing the original outlines of Boston as it had developed before the filling in of the Back Bay and the southern part of the harbor.

The British had just passed a new tax on tea, lead, glass, and paint. It was called the Townsend Acts. Bostonians organized to boycott, or quit buying, the taxed goods. Adams wrote a letter to gain support for the boycott. Paul Revere carried the letter to Philadelphia, Pennsylvania, and Charleston, South Carolina. Colonists thought that they could get this tax repealed as they had done with the Stamp Act.

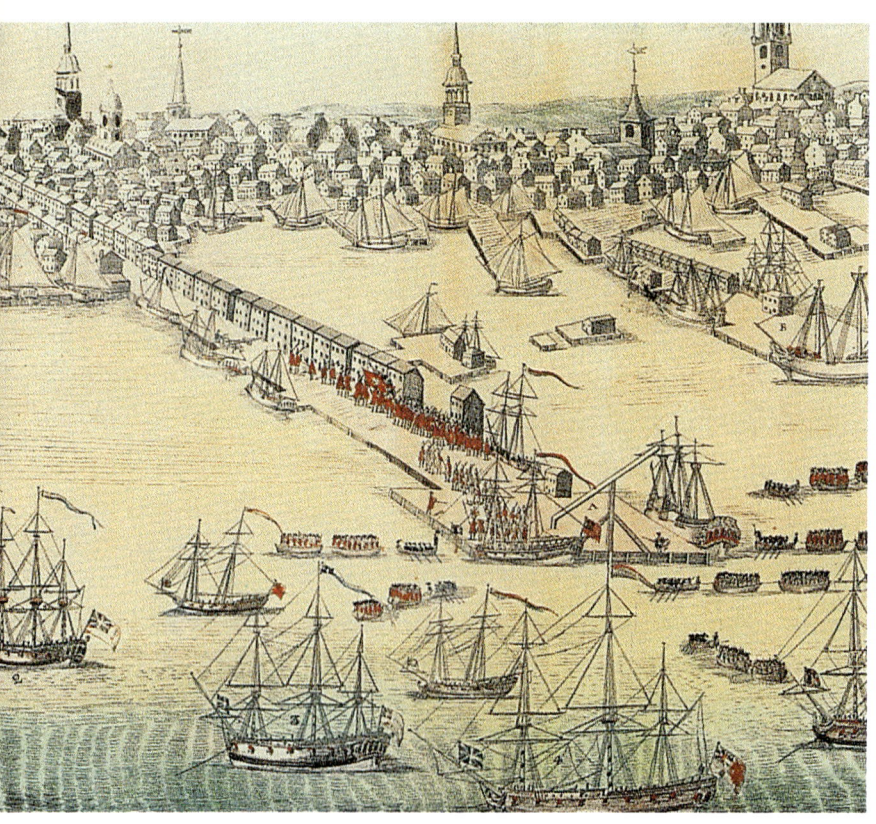

British troops land at Boston's Long Warf in 1768.

The British sent 4,000 redcoats to Boston.

The English, however, would not back down from the Townsend Acts. To enforce tax collection, the king sent 4,000 troops, dressed in uniforms of red coats, to camp on Boston Common. The "redcoats" were only three blocks from the Adams home. All day long Abigail had to listen to the marching soldiers as they drilled to the noise of fifes and drums.

Massacres and Tea Parties

TENSIONS GREW BETWEEN the Sons of Liberty and the redcoats. In March 1770, a small group of soldiers fired into a jeering crowd. Five colonists were killed and several others were wounded. Six soldiers were arrested. Samuel Adams asked the governor to remove the soldiers from Boston Common, which he did. The accused were then scheduled to be tried.

John was asked to represent the soldiers. He was worried that the Sons of Liberty would turn against him. But he believed everyone had the right to a lawyer in a trial. Adams called 96 witnesses before the court. At last someone said the soldiers were forced to fire. Adams pleaded for mercy. The jury found four of the soldiers not guilty. The other two soldiers were branded on the thumb as punishment.

Paul Revere's print depicting the Boston Massacre.

Samuel Adams called the shooting the Boston Massacre. But the case increased John's popularity as a lawyer. He had a large practice full of wealthy Bostonians. With fewer cases and larger fees, John moved the family back to Braintree. When John was gone, Abigail ran the house and the farm.

In 1773, Parliament repealed all taxes except the one on tea. Colonists continued to smuggle to avoid the three-cent tax per pound of tea. Parliament lowered the tariff, but most Americans still refused to buy the tea. Samuel Adams urged his followers not to allow any tea to be unloaded in Boston Harbor. John wrote Samuel's ideas down in newspaper articles.

One night, a group of 50 men dressed up as Indians. They ran to the Boston docks wearing blankets and feathers. As they shouted war whoops, the men raided three ships, then dumped 300 casks of tea into Boston Harbor. The incident became known as the Boston Tea Party. Paul Revere's riders spread news of the Tea Party throughout the colonies.

Colonists, some disguised as Mohawk Indians, dump British tea into Boston Harbor.

The First Continental Congress

THE BOSTON TEA PARTY caused the British to close Boston Harbor in 1773. Bostonians were forced to house British soldiers. Samuel Adams called for a meeting of colonists in Philadelphia. It was called the First Continental Congress.

On August 10, 1774, John and Samuel Adams went to Philadelphia with three other Massachusetts delegates. They rode over a muddy, rutted trail in a horse-drawn carriage. It was one of the first roads that linked cities in the colonies. Along the way, people came out to meet the delegates. They rang church bells and fired cannons in salute. There were feasts, parades, and parties. It took the men 19 days to reach Philadelphia.

Delegates leaving Carpenter's Hall, Philadelphia, site of the First Continental Congress.

The Adams cousins joined 48 other delegates in Carpenter's Hall on September 5, 1774. Assembled were some of the finest minds of the day. Some were wealthy landowners. Some were tradesmen or lawyers. All agreed that if England could hurt Boston, it could hurt every other city, town, and village.

The meeting went on for weeks as the delegates argued over what to do. Some, like John Adams, wanted a complete break with England. Others simply wanted a small amount of power. When the meeting broke up on October 28, the group had a list of demands they sent to King George. The Continental Congress wanted civil rights in the colonies. And they created a group of representatives from each colony to tighten the ban on English goods.

Carpenter's Hall, Philadelphia.

The Minutemen

BACK HOME ON THE FARM, the ban on English goods caused hardships for the Adams family. There was a shortage of food and supplies needed for farming. When the king saw the list of colonists' demands, he sent more soldiers to America. In every town Americans drilled to fight. They were called "minutemen" because they were ready to fight at a minute's notice. The men hid secret supplies of bullets and gunpowder.

On April 19, 1775, the redcoats began a march from Boston to Lexington and Concord, Massachusetts. This was barely 20 miles (32 km.) from the Adams home in Braintree. The redcoats were looking for hidden supplies of guns and power.

40 Founding Fathers

The minutemen and the redcoats clashed in Concord, leaving eight colonists dead. In Lexington, farmers, minutemen, and townsfolk pushed the British back to Boston. America and England were at war. John prepared for the long journey to Philadelphia, where the Continental Congress was called to meet once again.

American colonists and British soldiers exchange fire at the Battle of Lexington.

The Declaration of Independence

ADAMS WORKED HARD at the Continental Congress, usually from 7:00 a.m. until 10:00 p.m. He had to convince the other delegates of the wisdom of independence. He wanted to raise money for an army and a navy to fight the British. At the time, Boston soldiers had few supplies, relying on local farmers for food. Adams suggested George Washington as commander-in-chief of a Continental Army.

Congress would have to create a government to raise taxes, recruit soldiers, and deal with foreign countries. John proposed his plan for three branches of government elected by the people. On July 4, 1776, Adams and the other delegates put their name to The Declaration of Independence, written mainly by Thomas Jefferson. America claimed it was a free country no longer ruled by England.

Facing page: A copy of the United States Declaration of Independence.

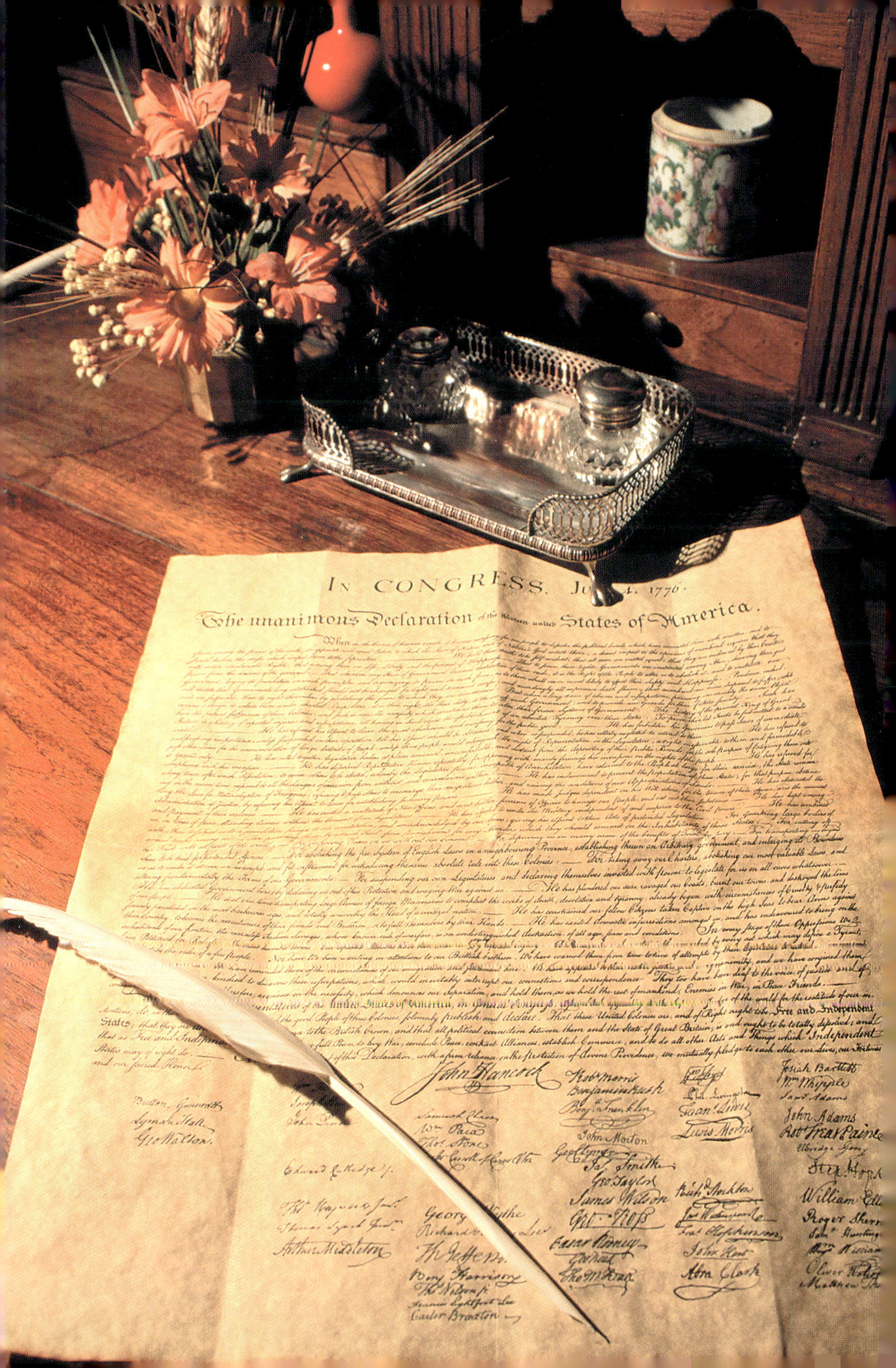
IN CONGRESS
The unanimous Declaration
States of America.

Off to France

BY NOVEMBER 1777, Adams was hoping to retire from politics. His law business was losing money, and his children were growing up without him. But duty called. Congress had appointed him to go to Paris, along with Benjamin Franklin and Arthur Lee. The men were to make peace with France. Crossing the sea to France took two months.

Shortly after Adams's arrival in Paris, France once again declared war on England and began helping the Americans. But Adams disliked France. And he felt he was too stubborn to be a diplomat. After 18 months in Paris, Adams returned to Braintree.

Congress had other plans for Adams. Within three months, he was ordered back to France. England was tiring of the war in America.

Congress hoped Adams could negotiate a peace treaty from Paris. But the war dragged on for three more years. Adams longed to return to his family.

As the years passed, John's sons, John Quincy and Charles joined him in Europe. John finally laid the foundation for peace between England and the United States. After years of hard fighting, George Washington and his troops had defeated the British. The war officially ended on September 3, 1783, when Adams, Benjamin Franklin, and John Jay signed a treaty in Paris.

Signing of the Peace Treaty, by painter Benjamin West. From left to right: John Jay, John Adams, Benjamin Franklin, Henry Laurens, and Franklin's grandson, William Temple Franklin. The British commissioners of the treaty refused to pose, and the picture was never finished.

John Adams 45

The Diplomat

WITH THE PEACE TREATY signed, Adams yearned to return to Braintree. Instead, he was ordered to negotiate trade treaties between 20 European nations, including England. Adams sent for his wife and daughter to join him in France. The family would be together for the first time in five years.

Adams was soon appointed as the first American minister to Great Britain. King George met with Adams in London. This was the first time the king had to receive an agent from the colonies. John thought the meeting went well.

Adams and his family lived in London for three years. Adams helped develop good relations between the two former enemies. Meanwhile, in the United States, delegates dissolved the

Continental Congress. They wrote a new document to run the country. It was called the Constitution. John Adams inspired many of the ideas in it.

John Adams, first American ambassador to the English Court, makes a presentation to King George III of England.

The First Vice-President

ADAMS HAD BEEN IN EUROPE for 10 years. Longing to return home, he resigned his post as minister to Great Britain. Much had changed in America. The Constitution guaranteed rights such as freedom of the press and freedom of religion.

After the Constitution was adopted, George Washington was elected first president. John Adams was elected as vice-president. He did not like being in second place, but Adams agreed to once more serve his country. On April 30, 1789, Adams was sworn in as the first vice-president. The Adamses moved into a manor house in New York City, the seat of government at the time.

Adams took the job very seriously. As the first vice-president, he knew his behavior could set custom for years to come. Still, he did not like the job. He wrote, "My country has in its wisdom contrived for me the most insignificant office that was ever the invention of man."

The vice-president, however, had an important task. He had to cast the deciding vote in the Senate in case of a tie. During his first term, Adams cast more tie-breaking votes than any other vice-president in history. Washington and Adams were elected to second terms in 1793.

John Adams watches off to the side as George Washington is inaugurated first president of the United States.

The Second President

IN ADAMS'S SECOND TERM, the government was moved from New York to Philadelphia. A new capital was being built on the swamps of the Potomac River across from Alexandria, Virginia. However, the new nation had little money. Adams received only $5,000 a year, with no living expenses. To save money, Abigail returned to Braintree.

Though Adams's first term had been calm, the second was not. England was once again at war with France. Both France and England were trying to drag America into their war. President Washington remained neutral.

George Washington refused to serve a third term as president. During his term, two political parties had emerged, the Federalists and the Republicans. The Federalists chose Adams as their candidate for president. The Republicans chose

A portrait of President John Adams.

Thomas Jefferson. When the votes were counted, John Adams was elected the second president of the United States.

Adams took the oath of office on March 4, 1797. He gave a moving speech. But the crowds came to applaud the outgoing president George Washington. With Abigail in Braintree, Adams lived alone in the three-story house that Congress had bought for the president in Philadelphia.

Troubles in Office

JOHN ADAMS' TERM AS PRESIDENT was marred by the deeds of foreign countries. France seized American sailors. They also refused peace agents and demanded money. To make matters worse, Adams was unpopular with his own Federalist Party. The Federalists hindered Adams' peace efforts with France.

The lonely president retreated to Braintree to be with his wife. From there, his orders were often ignored. Many Federalists wrote that Adams was unfit for the job. In the next election, in 1800, Thomas Jefferson was elected president. It was an ugly campaign. Though he was a healthy 65 years old, his enemies called him "old, bald, blind, crippled, toothless Adams."

Before his term was up, Adams moved his family to the newly built White House in

Washington, D.C. Abigail found it to be a "large and uncompleted castle in the midst of a barren swamp surrounded by forests." The White House was finished on the outside. Inside it lacked staircases, water, candles, and firewood for heat.

In 1799, when France and the United States were nearly at war, the American warship Constellation *(right) captured the French ship* L'Insurgente.

Retirement

WHEN THE REPUBLICANS took power, Adams doubted the Constitution would survive. He spent his last days in office appointing Federalists to key government positions. On the day of Jefferson's inauguration, Adams left the capital without saying a word. He would be the only president in history to refuse to greet his successor.

At the age of 65, John Adams was a bitter, tired man. After serving his country in Paris, Amsterdam, London, New York, Philadelphia, and Washington, he finally returned to Massachusetts. The area to which he moved was now called Quincy, after Abigail's grandfather. John and his wife of 37 years moved into a large home named Peacefield.

Adams's Federalist Party ignored him. But the people of Quincy treated him like royalty. Adams worked the farm and lived a productive life. He had 13 grandchildren and four great-grandchildren. Eventually Adams and Jefferson made peace with each other.

John Adams lived a productive life on his farm after serving his country as president.

Death of a President

THE ADAMSES CELEBRATED their 54th wedding anniversary in 1818. Abigail died three days later. John was filled with grief.

Adams's son, John Quincy Adams, was elected president in 1824. The country celebrated its 50th birthday during his term on July 4, 1826. John Quincy read the Constitution in a Washington, D.C. ceremony. In Massachusetts, his 91-year-old father lay dying. The old man opened his mouth to speak one more time. He said, "Thomas Jefferson survives." Then he died.

John Adams, however, was wrong. In a strange twist of fate, Thomas Jefferson had died a few hours earlier. The United States lost two great men on its 50th birthday. The second and third presidents were dead.

John Quincy Adams, John Adams's son, was elected president in 1824.

Conclusion

JOHN ADAMS OVERSAW the birth of the United States. He was not in the country during the Revolutionary War. But his work in Europe brought the United States status and recognition from foreign powers. He was brought down by political fighting in Congress. Through it all, he sacrificed for his country.

John Adams spent dozens of years separated from the wife and family he loved. Thanks to his wisdom, the American government has survived for more than two centuries. All Americans owe a great debt to their second president, John Adams.

Facing page: John Adams, in his last portrait, by Gilbert Stuart.

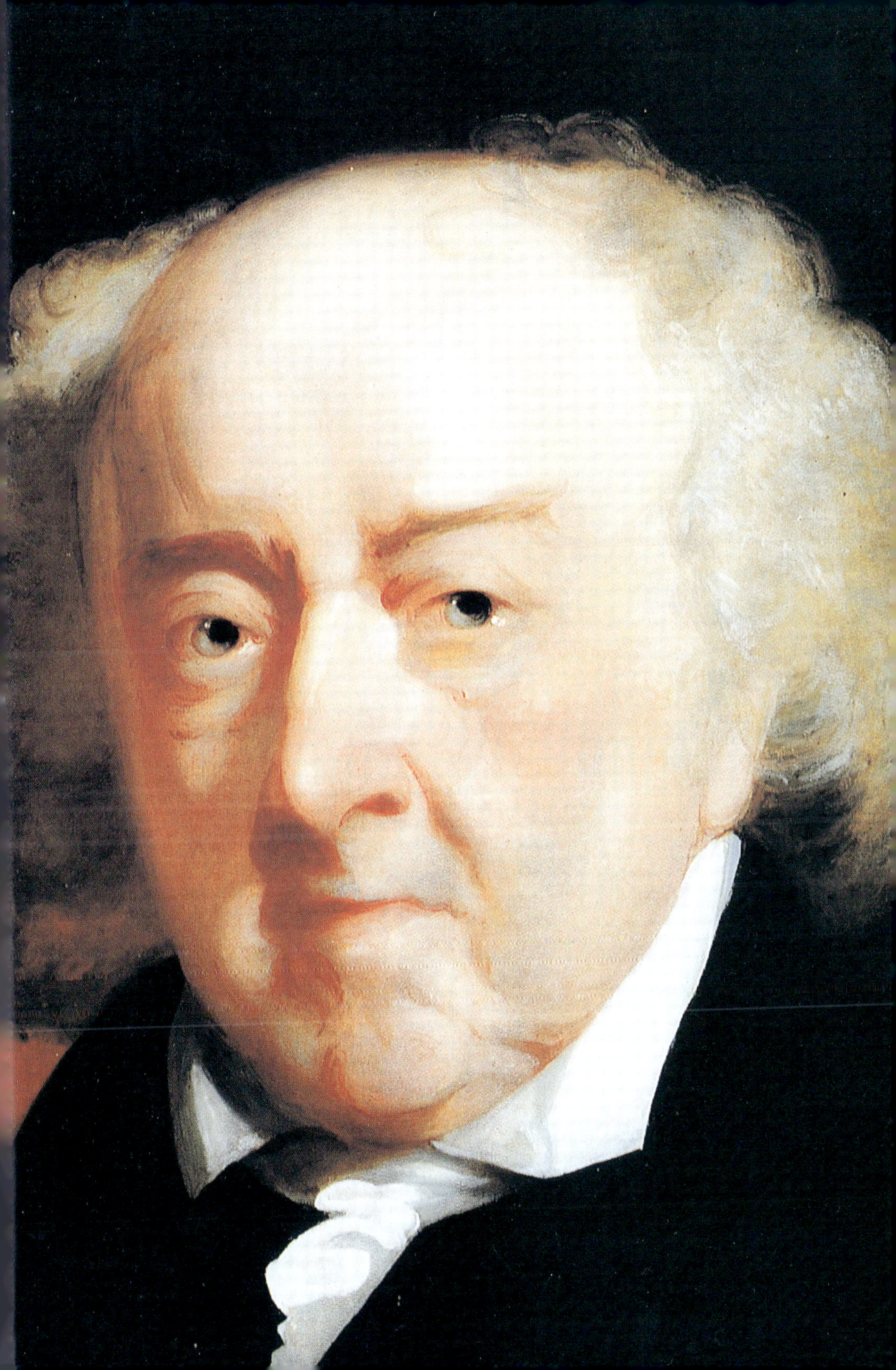

Timeline

October 30, 1735   John Adams born in Braintree, Massachusetts.

1755   Graduated from Harvard College.

Takes a teaching job in Worcester, Massachusetts. Continues his studies in Latin, history, and law.

1758   Begins a law practice in Braintree. Becomes respected as a good lawyer, first in Braintree and later in Boston.

1764   Marries Abigail Smith. The couple have five children, including John Quincy Adams, who goes on to become the sixth president of the United States.

1764-68   Argues against Stamp Act and Townsend Acts.

1770   Defends British soldiers in court after Boston Massacre.

1773   Supports Boston Tea Party.

1774   Delegate to First Continental Congress.

1775   Delegate to Second Continental Congress. Helps write United States Declaration of Independence.

1777-1788   Diplomat in France, Netherlands, and England.

1789   First vice president of the United States. Serves two terms.

1797   Second president of the United States. Serves one term, then finally retires from public life, moving back to Braintree (now called Quincy).

July 4, 1826   John Adams dies, the same day as Thomas Jefferson.

Where on the Web?

Adams National Historical Park
http://www.nps.gov/adam/

American Presidents Life Portraits
http://www.americanpresidents.org/presidents/president.asp?PresidentNumber=2

Internet Public Library
http://www.ipl.org/ref/POTUS/jadams.html

John Adams: Unsung Hero of the American Revolution
http://www.universalway.org/johnadams.html

Mr. President: Profiles of our Nation's Leaders
http://web7.si.edu/president/gallery/detail.cfm?prez_ID=2

John Adams: Second President of the United States
http://library.thinkquest.org/12587/contents/personalities/jadams/ja.html?tqskip=1

Glossary

American Revolution: the war between Great Britain and its American colonies that lasted from 1775 to 1783. America won its independence in the war.

Bill of Rights: a statement of citizen's rights that make up the first 10 amendments to the United States Constitution. Some of the amendments guarantee free speech, protection from search and seizure, and the right of a militia to bear arms.

boycott: to try to change the actions of a company or government by refusing to buy their products.

The Colonies: the British territories that made up the first 13 states of the United States. The 13 colonies were the states of New Hampshire, Massachusetts, Rhode Island, Connecticut, New York, New Jersey, Pennsylvania, Delaware, Maryland, Virginia, North Carolina, South Carolina, and Georgia.

Constitution: the document that spells out the principles and laws that govern the United States.

Constitutional Convention: the meeting of men who wrote the United States Constitution.

Continental Army: the army that fought the British in the Revolutionary War.

Continental Congress: lawmakers who governed the 13 colonies after they declared their independence from Great Britain.

Declaration of Independence: the document written by Thomas Jefferson that declared America's independence from Great Britain.

Federalist: a political party that favors a strong central government over the states.

House of Representatives: a governing body elected by popular vote to rule a nation.

legislature: a body of persons with the power to make, change, or repeal laws.

militia: a body of citizens enrolled in military service during a time of emergency.

tariff: a tax placed by a government on imported goods.

Index

A
Adams, Abigail 22, 23, 24, 26, 31, 34, 46, 50, 51, 53, 54, 56
Adams, Charles 45
Adams, Henry 8
Adams, John Quincy 28, 45, 54, 56
Adams, Samuel 24, 28, 32, 34, 36
Alexandria, VA 50
Amsterdam, Netherlands 54

B
Boston, MA 8, 15, 16, 21, 24, 26, 28, 30, 31, 32, 34, 36, 38, 40, 41, 42
Boston Common 31, 32
Boston Gazette 26
Boston Harbor 34, 36
Boston Massacre 34
Braintree, MA 8, 10, 15, 21, 34, 40, 44, 46, 50, 51, 52
Brattle Square 28

C
Carpenter's Hall 38
Charleston, S.C. 30
Concord, MA 40, 41
Congress 4, 36, 38, 41, 42, 44, 45, 47, 51, 58
Constitution 47, 48, 54, 56
Continental Army 42
Continental Congress 36, 38, 41, 42, 47

D
Declaration of Independence 42

E
England 4, 6, 8, 14, 16, 18, 21, 24, 26, 38, 41, 42, 44, 45, 46, 50

F
Federalist 6, 50, 52, 54
First Continental Congress 36
France 4, 6, 14, 16, 44, 46, 50, 52
Franklin, Benjamin 44, 45

G
Great Britain 46, 48

H
Harvard 11, 12, 14

J
Jay, John 45
Jefferson, Thomas 42, 51, 52, 54, 56

K
King George III 16, 21, 38, 46

L
Lee, Arthur 44
Lexington, MA 40, 41
London, England 46, 54

M
Massachusetts 8, 9, 11, 12, 26, 28, 36, 40, 54, 56
minutemen 40, 41

N
New York City 48, 50, 54

O
Otis, James 21

P
Paris, France 44, 45, 54
Parliament 18, 24, 26, 34
Peacefield 54
Pennsylvania 30
Philadelphia, PA 30, 36, 41, 50, 51, 54
Plymouth, MA 8
Potomac River 50
Puritan 8, 9, 14
Putnam, James 15

R
Republican 6, 50, 54
Revere, Paul 30, 34
Revolutionary War 58

S
Senate 49
Sons of Liberty 24, 28, 32
South Carolina 30
Stamp Act 24, 26, 30
Stamp Tax 26

T
Townsend Acts 30, 31

U
United States 45, 46, 51, 56, 58

V
Virginia 50

W
Washington, D.C. 53, 54, 56
Washington, George 42, 45, 48, 49, 50, 51
White House 52, 53
Worcester, MA 12, 14, 15

64 Founding Fathers